JACKSONVILLE JAGUARS

BRENDAN FLYNN

WWW.APEXEDITIONS.COM

Apex is distributed by North Star Editions:
sales@northstareditions.com | 888-417-0195

Produced for Apex by Red Line Editorial.

Photographs ©: Logan Bowles/AP Images, cover, 1; Phelan M. Ebenhack/AP Images, 4–5; John Raoux/AP Images, 6–7, 36–37, 58–59; Focus on Sport/Getty Images Sport/Getty Images, 8–9; Allen Kee/Getty Images Sport/Getty Images, 10–11; Mark Duncan/AP Images, 12–13; Chris Stanford/Hulton Archive/Getty Images, 14–15; George Gojkovich/Getty Images Sport/Getty Images, 16–17; Al Messerschmidt/AP Images, 19, 26–27, 57; Jim McIsaac/Getty Images Sport/Getty Images, 20–21; Scott Cunningham/Getty Images Sport/Getty Images, 22–23; Rick Stewart/Getty Images Sport/Getty Images, 24–25; Sam Greenwood/Getty Images Sport/Getty Images, 29, 32–33, 34–35; Maddie Meyer/Getty Images Sport/Getty Images, 30–31; Peter Nicholls/Getty Images Sport/Getty Images, 38–39; Mike Carlson/Getty Images Sport/Getty Images, 40–41, 42–43, 47, 48–49; Jonathan Bachman/Getty Images Sport/Getty Images, 44–45; Matthew Ashton/AMA/Corbis Sport/Getty Images, 50–51; Cindy Marshall/AP Images, 52–53; Don Juan Moore/Getty Images Sport/Getty Images, 54–55

Library of Congress Control Number: 2023922692

ISBN
979-8-89250-085-2 (hardcover)
979-8-89250-102-6 (paperback)
979-8-89250-135-4 (ebook pdf)
979-8-89250-119-4 (hosted ebook)

Printed in the United States of America
Mankato, MN
082024

NOTE TO PARENTS AND EDUCATORS

Apex books are designed to build literacy skills in striving readers. Exciting, high-interest content attracts and holds readers' attention. The text is carefully leveled to allow students to achieve success quickly.

TABLE OF CONTENTS

CHAPTER 1

DUUUVAL!

It's game day in Jacksonville, Florida. Fans wearing teal and black fill the stands. Some greet one another with high fives. Others throw their heads back and shout "Duuuval!" It's a cheer known to all true Jaguars fans.

Jaguars fans go crazy as the players run onto the field.

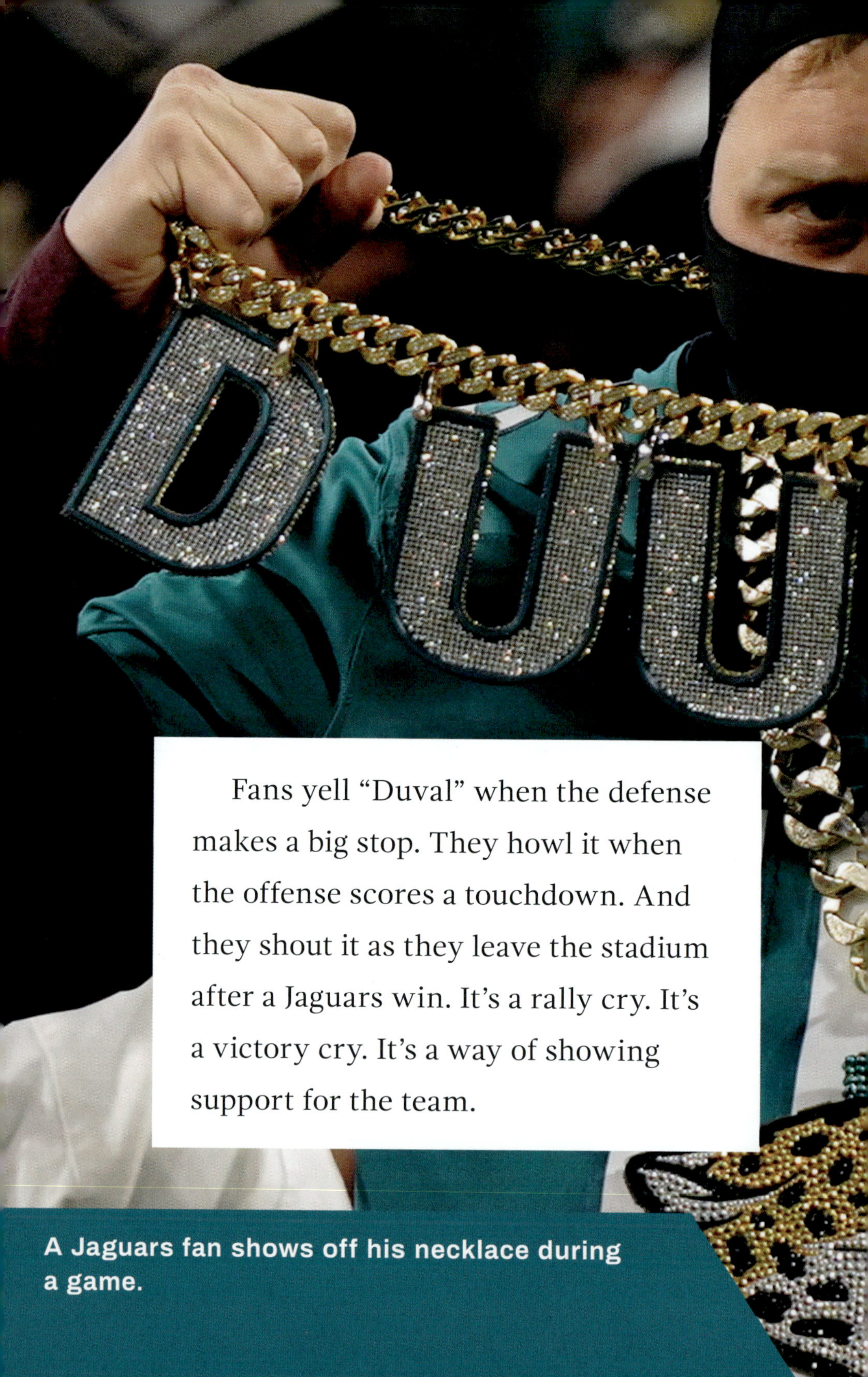

Fans yell “Duval” when the defense makes a big stop. They howl it when the offense scores a touchdown. And they shout it as they leave the stadium after a Jaguars win. It’s a rally cry. It’s a victory cry. It’s a way of showing support for the team.

A Jaguars fan shows off his necklace during a game.

WHY DUVAL?

Jacksonville is in Duval County in northern Florida. In the early 1990s, rappers from the area started referring to their home as Duval. "Duval" caught on with Jaguars fans. They have been shouting it ever since.

CHAPTER 2

EARLY HISTORY

The Jacksonville Jaguars began play in 1995. They were an expansion team. They joined the NFL along with the Carolina Panthers. The Jaguars became the third NFL team in Florida. The Miami Dolphins were the first. The Tampa Bay Buccaneers were the second.

The Jaguars played their first game against the Houston Oilers. The Jaguars lost that game, but they beat Houston later in the season.

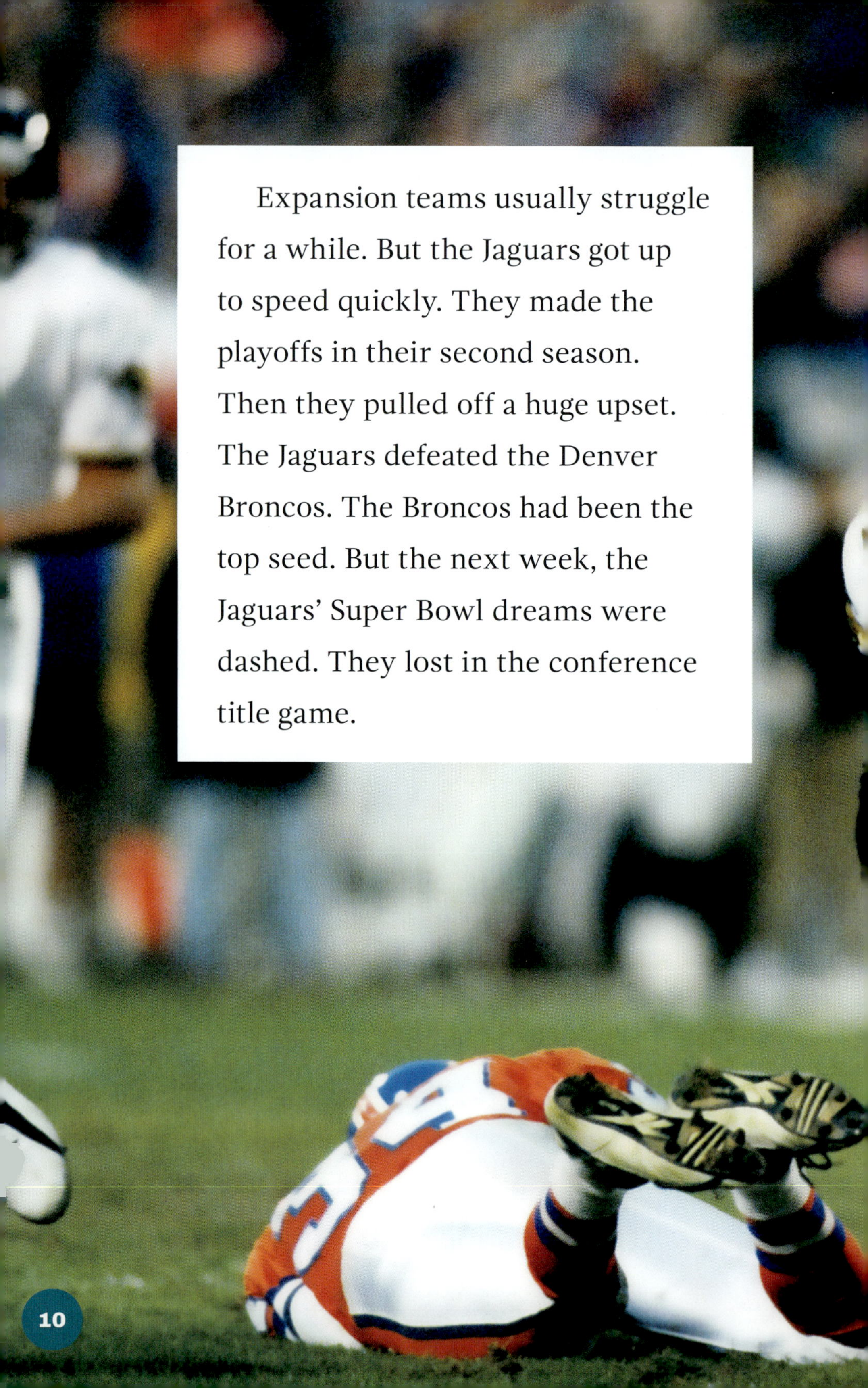

Expansion teams usually struggle for a while. But the Jaguars got up to speed quickly. They made the playoffs in their second season. Then they pulled off a huge upset. The Jaguars defeated the Denver Broncos. The Broncos had been the top seed. But the next week, the Jaguars' Super Bowl dreams were dashed. They lost in the conference title game.

Natrone Means (20) dives for extra yards during Jacksonville's playoff game against the Denver Broncos.

Jaguars quarterback Mark Brunell leaps into the end zone during a 1999 game against the Cleveland Browns.

The Jaguars showed their success wasn't a fluke. They reached the playoffs in each of the next three seasons. That included two division titles. In 1999, they put together an 11-game winning streak. Their 14–2 record was the best in the NFL that year.

GATOR BOWL

The Gator Bowl has been a major college bowl game since 1946. It is played in Jacksonville. The Gator Bowl stadium was torn down in 1994. The Jaguars' stadium was built on the same site. It became the new home of the Gator Bowl game.

The Jaguars opened the 1999 playoffs against the Miami Dolphins. The Jaguars rolled to a 62–7 win. They reached the conference title game. There, they hosted the Tennessee Titans. The Titans had beaten the Jaguars twice in the regular season. Those had been the Jaguars' only two losses that year. The Titans made it three with a 33–14 win. Just as in 1996, the Jaguars fell one game short of the Super Bowl.

Running back James Stewart (33) pounds his way through the Miami Dolphins defense during a playoff game.

In the 2007 season, Jacksonville beat the Pittsburgh Steelers 31–29 in the first round of the playoffs.

The next few years were rough. The Jaguars didn't return to the playoffs until 2005. That season, they lost to the New England Patriots in the first round. Two years later, the Jaguars made it to the second round. But the next week, the Patriots ended their season again.

BACK IN THE DAY

The Jaguars weren't the first pro football team in Jacksonville. In 1974, the Sharks played there. And the Express played there the following year. Both teams were part of the World Football League. The Jacksonville Bulls were part of the United States Football League in 1984 and 1985.

PLAYER SPOTLIGHT

MARK BRUNELL

Quarterback Mark Brunell won the starting job early in the Jaguars' first season. In 1996, he led the NFL with 4,367 passing yards. Then he carried the Jaguars in their upset against Denver. The Jaguars trailed 12–0 early in the game. But Brunell responded. He led six straight scoring drives.

Brunell remained a huge part of the team for eight seasons. He made the Pro Bowl three times. Brunell was the third player in the team's ring of honor.

MARK BRUNELL THREW FOR MORE THAN 25,000 YARDS IN HIS NINE YEARS WITH THE JAGUARS.

Riddell
Wilson

CHAPTER 3

LEGENDS

Fred Taylor was the Jaguars' first star running back. He was a rookie in 1998. Maurice Jones-Drew arrived in 2006. He racked up 1,606 rushing yards in 2011. That led the NFL.

Maurice Jones-Drew scores a touchdown against the New York Jets in 2009.

David Garrard tossed 89 touchdown passes during his nine-year career.

Mark Brunell led the Jaguars to four playoff appearances. In 2003, the team drafted Byron Leftwich. He replaced Brunell. Leftwich was solid when healthy. But he struggled with injuries. David Garrard was a longtime backup quarterback. He stepped up when Leftwich got hurt. Garrard started for five seasons.

TOUGH COACH

Tom Coughlin was Jacksonville's first head coach. He also decided which players to add to the team. Coughlin demanded a lot from his players. But he taught them discipline. This helped make them winners.

Tony Boselli made the Pro Bowl five years in a row from 1996 to 2000.

Jacksonville's early playoff teams had two great wide receivers. Jimmy Smith recorded 116 catches in 1999. That led the league. Smith had at least 1,000 receiving yards in nine seasons. Keenan McCardell excelled from 1996 to 2001. In those seasons, he averaged more than 1,000 receiving yards per year.

HALL OF FAMER

Offensive tackle Tony Boselli was the team's first draft pick. He went No. 2 overall in the 1995 NFL Draft. Boselli starred on the Jaguars for six seasons. He became the first Jaguar to enter the Pro Football Hall of Fame.

Kevin Hardy recorded more than 500 tackles during his six years with Jacksonville.

Kevin Hardy became the team's first defensive star. The linebacker was a first-team All-Pro in 1999. Defensive linemen Marcus Stroud and John Henderson kept opposing running backs in check. Cornerback Rashean Mathis spent 10 seasons in Jacksonville. He became the team's all-time interception leader.

LEADING THE DEFENSE

Linebacker Paul Posluszny joined the Jaguars in 2011. He was the team's defensive leader for the next seven seasons. His best year came in 2013. He led the NFL with 122 solo tackles. He also made the Pro Bowl.

PLAYER SPOTLIGHT

FRED TAYLOR

When the Jaguars needed to get tough yards, they often called on Fred Taylor. The running back burst out of the gate in 1998. As a rookie, he rushed for 1,223 yards. He also scored 17 touchdowns.

Taylor was a fixture in the backfield for 10 years. He rushed for at least 1,000 yards in seven seasons. He helped out in the passing game, too. Injuries often kept him on the sideline. Even so, he set several team records.

FRED TAYLOR SCORED 70 TOUCHDOWNS DURING HIS 11 YEARS WITH THE JAGUARS.

Riddell
28
C
28
Wilson

CHAPTER 4

RECENT HISTORY

After the mid-2000s, the Jaguars hit a slump. From 2008 to 2016, they suffered one of their worst stretches. They missed the playoffs nine years in a row. The seasons from 2011 to 2016 were especially tough. Jacksonville won no more than five games each of those years.

Allen Robinson makes a great touchdown catch during a 2016 game against the Baltimore Ravens.

In 2017, the Jaguars earned the nickname "Sacksonville" because of how often defenders brought down quarterbacks.

In 2017, the Jaguars bounced back. Midway through the season, they won seven of eight games. They finished the season 10–6. Next, the Jaguars beat the Buffalo Bills in the first round of the playoffs. After that, they shocked the Pittsburgh Steelers. Jacksonville won 45–42. But the Jaguars lost in the conference title game. Once again, they fell to the Patriots.

The success of the 2017 season didn't last. Over the next four years, Jacksonville won a total of just 15 games. That included a 1–15 finish in 2020. The next year wasn't much better. The Jaguars won only three games.

FIRST-ROUND PICKS

The Jaguars' one-win season in 2020 had a bright spot. They received the first overall pick in the 2021 draft. They selected quarterback Trevor Lawrence. The Jaguars had another first-round pick that year. They used it on running back Travis Etienne. He had been Lawrence's college teammate.

Jaguars quarterback Blake Bortles fires a pass during a 2018 game.

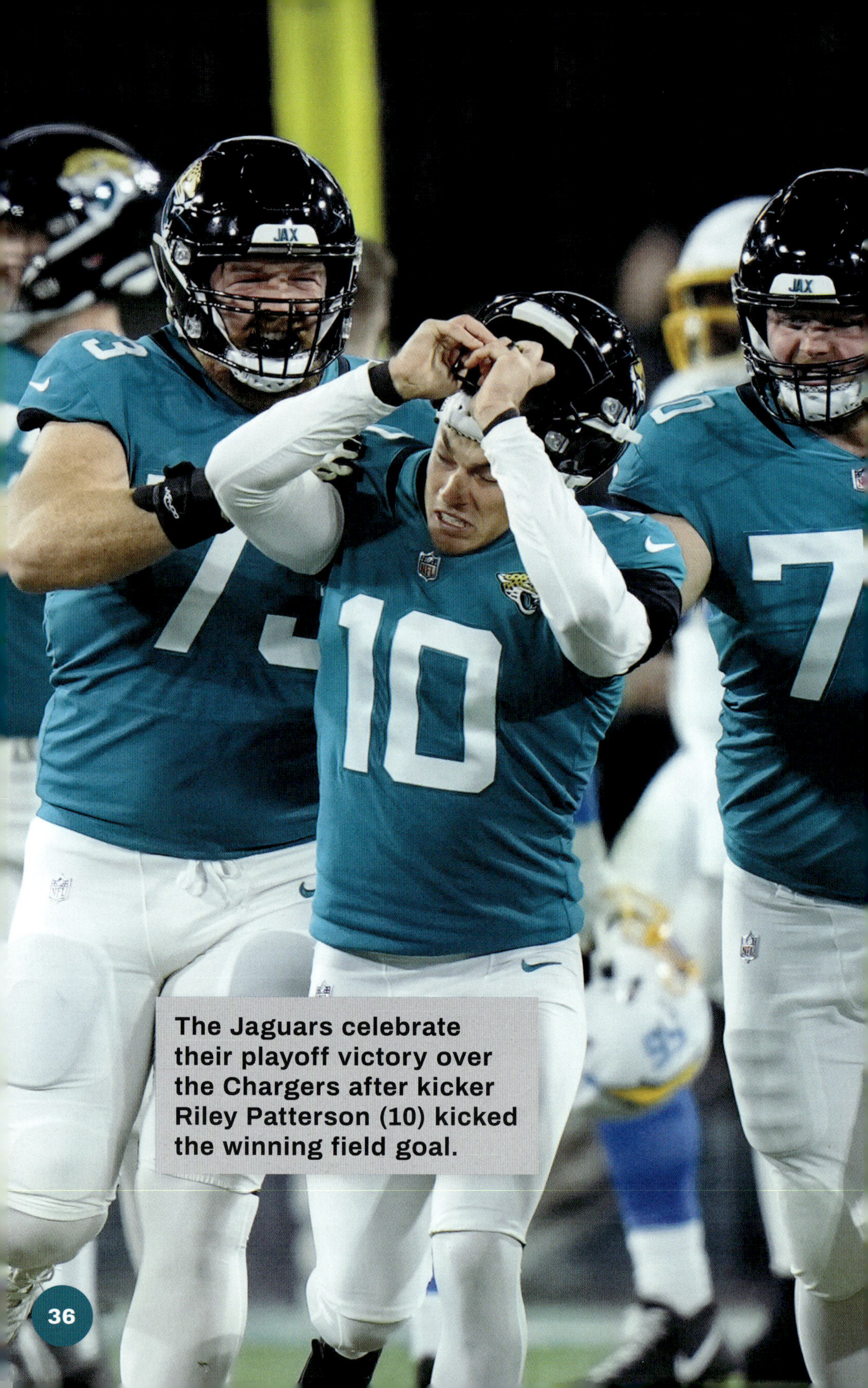

The Jaguars celebrate their playoff victory over the Chargers after kicker Riley Patterson (10) kicked the winning field goal.

In 2021, rookie Trevor Lawrence took over at quarterback. In his second year, he led the Jaguars back to the playoffs. They won their first-round playoff game. They beat the Los Angeles Chargers 31–30. The Jaguars lost a close game in the next round. But it was a positive sign for the future.

CAPTAIN COMEBACK

Lawrence had a wild day in the playoffs against the Chargers. He threw four interceptions in the first half. The Jaguars fell behind 27–0. But Lawrence turned things around in the second half. He threw four touchdown passes. Then the Jaguars kicked a last-second field goal. That sealed the dramatic win.

CHAPTER 5

MODERN STARS

Trevor Lawrence got off to a fast start in 2021. He threw 602 passes. That was the third most of all time for a rookie. Travis Etienne took over at running back in 2022. He rushed for more than 1,000 yards that year. He topped 1,000 yards again in 2023.

Travis Etienne piled up more than 2,900 total yards in his first two years with the Jaguars.

Marcedes Lewis was a Jaguar from 2006 until 2017. The tight end's best year came in 2010. He hauled in 10 touchdown passes. He made the Pro Bowl, too. Wide receiver Allen Robinson made the Pro Bowl in 2015. He notched 14 touchdown catches. In 2022, Evan Engram joined the team. The tight end caught 114 passes in 2023. That was the second most of all time for a tight end.

FLORIDA FAVORITE

Quarterback Blake Bortles was a fan favorite. In 2017, the Florida native led the Jaguars to the playoffs. It was their only playoff appearance in a 14-year span.

Evan Engram jumps into the crowd after scoring a touchdown in 2023.

Defensive end Calais Campbell joined the Jaguars in 2017. He had three Pro Bowl seasons with the team. In 2023, linebacker Josh Allen made his second Pro Bowl. He made a powerful duo with linebacker Travon Walker. Together, Allen and Walker recorded 27.5 sacks. That was the most for a pair in 2023.

ONE FOR THE BOOKS

In 2021, Jamal Agnew tied a record that can never be broken. A long field goal try fell short. Agnew caught the ball in the back of the end zone. He returned it 109 yards for a touchdown. It's tied for the longest return in NFL history.

Travon Walker (left) and Josh Allen (right) take down Baltimore Ravens quarterback Lamar Jackson.

Cornerback Jalen Ramsey finished second in Rookie of the Year voting in 2016. The next year, he was a first-team All-Pro pick. He shut down some of the top receivers in the game. Linebacker Myles Jack had more than 100 tackles three times between 2018 and 2021. In 2022, Foyesade Oluokun led the league in solo tackles. He did it again in 2023.

STARTING OFF STRONG

Doug Pederson was hired as the Jaguars' head coach in 2022. Pederson had won a Super Bowl title with the Philadelphia Eagles. In his first year with Jacksonville, he took the team to the playoffs.

Foyesade Oluokun (23) returns an interception for a touchdown during a 2023 game against the New Orleans Saints.

PLAYER SPOTLIGHT

TREVOR LAWRENCE

Trevor Lawrence led Clemson to a national title as a freshman in college. He paired his quick release with a powerful arm. The Jaguars hoped he'd have the same success in the NFL. In his first game, he threw for 332 yards. Lawrence also tossed three touchdown passes. He remained the starter the rest of the season.

However, Lawrence really took off in his second year. He threw for more than 4,000 yards. He tossed 25 touchdown passes as well. With those numbers, he earned his first trip to the Pro Bowl.

IN 2023, TREVOR LAWRENCE TOPPED 4,000 PASSING YARDS FOR THE SECOND TIME.

JAX
16
C
NFL
16
16

CHAPTER 6

TEAM TRIVIA

The team's first logo showed a leaping jaguar. However, the Jaguar car company sued Jacksonville. The team hadn't even played a game yet. But the company said the leaping jaguar was too similar to its own logo. So, the Jaguars had to change their logo. The team's new logo showed a snarling jaguar's head.

A Jaguars flag-waver fires up the crowd before a game.

In 2007, the NFL started playing regular-season games in London, England. No team has played there more than the Jaguars. Entering 2024, Jacksonville had played 11 games in London.

The Jaguars have played several games at Wembley Stadium, which is the largest stadium in England.

SHAHID KHAN

Shahid Khan bought the Jaguars in 2012. He is one reason the team has played in London so often. Khan also owns a soccer club based in London.

The Jaguars added swimming pools to their stadium in 2014.

Some Jaguars fans can beat the heat at home games. The stadium has two swimming pools. Each one holds up to 20 people. Fans can splash in the pools while they're watching the game below.

FLOATING HOTELS

Jacksonville hosted the Super Bowl in the 2004 season. The big game always brings in thousands of fans and reporters. The city didn't have enough hotel rooms to meet the need. So, five cruise ships docked in the Saint Johns River. Some visitors stayed there.

In 2012, a fan club for the Jaguars formed. It was called the Bold City Brigade. Before games, the group gets together. People gather at a place called the Slab. Fans gather outside Jacksonville, too. Fans from all over join in their love for the Jaguars.

A POOL OF MAYO

The Bold City Brigade can get rowdy. One year, the group brought a kiddie pool. Fans filled it with mayonnaise. Then they jumped into the pool. One fan proposed to his girlfriend afterward. He was still covered in mayo.

The Jaguars' slogan is "It was always the Jags." Fans often say it after the team wins.

TEAM RECORDS

All-Time Passing Yards: 25,698
Mark Brunell (1995–2003)

All-Time Touchdown Passes: 144
Mark Brunell (1995–2003)

All-Time Rushing Yards: 11,271
Fred Taylor (1998–2008)

All-Time Rushing Touchdowns: 68
Maurice Jones-Drew (2006–13)

All-Time Receiving Yards: 12,287
Jimmy Smith (1995–2005)

All-Time Interceptions: 30
Rashean Mathis (2003–12)

All-Time Sacks: 55
Tony Brackens (1996–2003)

All-Time Scoring: 1,022
Josh Scobee (2004–14)

All-Time Coaching Wins: 68
Tom Coughlin (1995–2002) and Jack Del Rio (2003–11)

All-Time Games Played: 209
Brad Meester (2000–13)

All statistics are accurate through 2023.

Riddell
NFL
Wilson

TIMELINE

1995
The Jacksonville Jaguars play their first game.

1996
In their second year, the Jaguars shock the NFL by reaching the playoffs and upsetting the top-seeded Broncos.

1999
The Jaguars earn the top playoff seed but lose to the Tennessee Titans in the conference championship game.

2002
Head coach Tom Coughlin is fired after his eighth season in Jacksonville.

2003
Injuries force tackle Tony Boselli, the team's first-ever draft pick, to retire at age 31.

2005: The Jaguars earn a playoff spot with a 12–4 record, but they lose in the first round.

2007: The Jaguars beat the Steelers to advance to the second round of the playoffs.

2017: Blake Bortles leads a surprise run to the conference championship game, but the Jaguars lose to the Patriots.

2021: The Jaguars select quarterback Trevor Lawrence with the first pick of the NFL Draft.

2022: Lawrence and rookie running back Travis Etienne lead the Jaguars to a division title.

COMPREHENSION QUESTIONS

Write your answers on a separate piece of paper.

1. Write a paragraph that explains the main ideas of Chapter 2.

2. Who do you think was the greatest player in Jacksonville Jaguars history? Why?

3. Which quarterback replaced Mark Brunell as the Jaguars' starter?

A. Blake Bortles
B. Trevor Lawrence
C. Byron Leftwich

4. Why was it a huge upset when the Jaguars beat the Denver Broncos in the 1996 playoffs?

A. The Broncos were considered a much better team.
B. The Jaguars didn't have a healthy quarterback.
C. The Jaguars and Broncos had a long rivalry.

5. What does **dashed** mean in this book?

But the next week, the Jaguars' Super Bowl dreams were ***dashed****. They lost in the conference title game.*

A. improved

B. ruined

C. ignored

6. What does **fixture** mean in this book?

Taylor was a ***fixture*** *in the backfield for 10 years. He rushed for at least 1,000 yards in seven seasons.*

A. big problem

B. steady player

C. short-lived star

Answer key on page 64.

GLOSSARY

conference
A group of teams that make up part of a sports league.

discipline
The practice of working hard and following rules.

division
In the NFL, a group of teams that make up part of a conference.

dramatic
Sudden and striking.

expansion team
A new team that is added to a league.

fluke
An unlikely chance event, especially a surprising piece of luck.

interception
A pass that is caught by a defensive player.

playoffs
A set of games played after the regular season to decide which team is the champion.

sacks
Plays that happen when a defender tackles the quarterback before he can throw the ball.

seed
A team's ranking heading into a tournament.

upset
When a team wins a game that it was expected to lose.

TO LEARN MORE

BOOKS

Coleman, Ted. *Jacksonville Jaguars All-Time Greats*. Mendota Heights, MN: Press Box Books, 2022.

Smith, Elliott. *Football's Best Traditions and Weirdest Superstitions*. North Mankato, MN: Capstone Press, 2023.

Stabler, David. *Meet Trevor Lawrence: Jacksonville Jaguars Superstar*. Minneapolis: Lerner Publications, 2024.

ONLINE RESOURCES

Visit **www.apexeditions.com** to find links and resources related to this title.

ABOUT THE AUTHOR

Brendan Flynn is a San Francisco resident and an author of numerous children's books. In addition to writing about sports, Flynn also enjoys competing in triathlons, Scrabble tournaments, and chili cook-offs.

INDEX

ANSWER KEY:

1. Answers will vary; 2. Answers will vary; 3. C; 4. A; 5. B; 6. B